Measure the Weather

by Cara Torrance

OXFORD
UNIVERSITY PRESS
AUSTRALIA & NEW ZEALAND

What We Measure and Why

We measure different kinds of information that relate to weather. We measure rainfall, water levels in oceans, lakes and rivers, air temperature and wind speed.

This information is important to us in our daily lives. It helps us in many ways, from planning how to dress for the day to deciding what crops to plant and when.

It is good to plan ahead for a wet day!

Measuring the weather helps us understand complex issues in our world. Weather information about natural disasters such as **drought** or flood allow us to plan for them. Weather information helps farmers know when to plant and harvest crops. It also tells us how weather patterns are changing and what this might mean for us in our daily lives.

Rainfall

How do we measure rainfall?

Rainfall is the amount of rain that falls in one place in a certain amount of time. We use a **udometer** to measure rainfall. It tells us how much rain falls in an area of 1 square metre over a certain period of time.

There are different kinds of udometers. The simplest udometer is a measuring cylinder udometer. A funnel-shaped collector catches the rain as it falls. The collector is attached to a measuring tube.

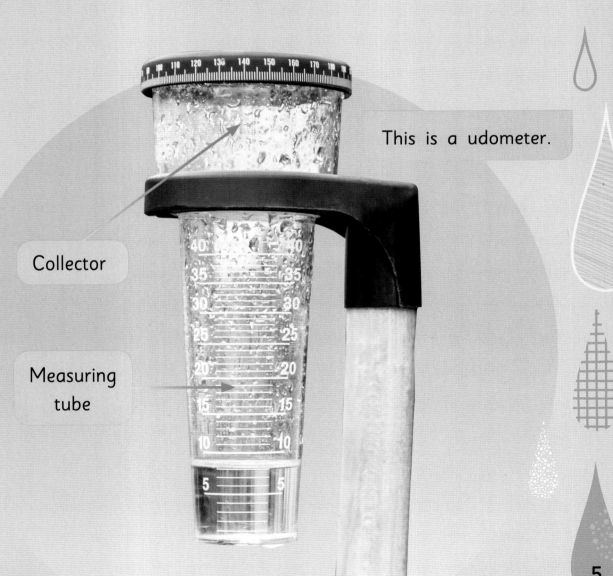

This is a udometer.

Collector

Measuring tube

Why do we measure rainfall?

It is important to measure rainfall. We can use the information to help us know when there might be water **shortages** or floods. Both water shortages and floods can result in disaster. Knowing about them early can help us plan for them.

A severe flood is a natural disaster, which can affect many people's lives.

Farmers can use information on rainfall to help them manage when to plant and harvest crops. Rainfall information can help farmers plan how to care for the land and animals in floods or droughts.

The information can also help us know when to restrict water. It can show whether the amount of rain falling is normal for the time of the year. In this way, we start to see if weather patterns are changing and new patterns are forming.

Rainfall is critical for farmers growing crops.

Water Levels

How do we measure water levels?

We can measure water levels in different ways. They are all complex. One way to measure ocean levels, or the height of the ocean, is with **satellites**.

You cannot just put a ruler in the ocean to measure the level.

The US space organisation, NASA, uses a satellite system to gather information about oceans. A satellite in space sends **radio waves** to the ocean. Scientists then measure the distance between the ocean and the satellite. This information is collected across the globe every ten days.

The Jason 3 is one of the satellites that gathers information about ocean levels.

satellite

ocean

Why do we measure water levels?

Monitoring and measuring water levels can show short-term changes. This helps us to act quickly when we need to. For example, measuring water levels in lakes, rivers and oceans helps us know when flooding might happen. This can help with keeping damage to a minimum and can even save lives.

Information about water levels also tells us when water storages in dams might run out.

If people know in time, they can get to safety.

Monitoring water levels over time can show changing weather patterns. Changes in ocean levels are the clearest indicator of this.

St Mark's Square in Venice, Italy, now often floods at high tide.

Wind Speed and Direction

How do we measure wind speed and direction?

How fast is the air moving? We have tools that can tell us. They measure wind speed and direction. They also record the strength of wind **gusts**. An **anemometer** measures wind speed in miles or kilometres per hour, or in **knots**. It measures direction in degrees to tell whether the wind is coming from the north, south, east or west.

A cup anemometer measures wind speed. Wind blows into three or four cups on a rod, causing the rod to turn at the speed of the wind.

A weather vane measures wind direction. It points in the direction the wind is coming from.

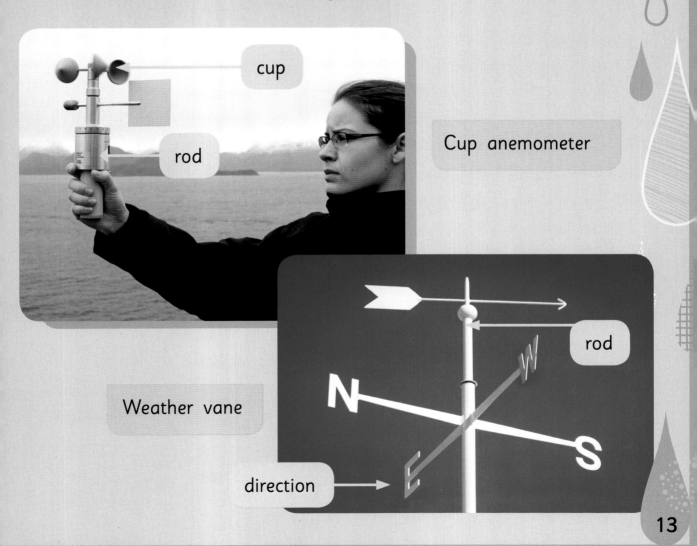

cup

rod

Cup anemometer

rod

Weather vane

N

W

S

E

direction

Why do we measure wind speed and direction?

Measuring wind speed can give us information that helps us plan what we do. For example, sailors must pay attention to wind speeds and weather forecasts to stay safe.

Weather can change quickly at sea, so it is important to plan and have current information.

Information about wind speed and direction helps us understand how quickly **weather systems** are moving and how severe they are. This can help us understand the damage that might occur and what to do. We can secure things around our homes or know when we should leave. Gathering information about wind helps us learn if weather patterns are changing. It can tell us if storms are getting stronger over time.

Wind can cause dangerous storm surges, which can do a lot of damage.

Air Temperature

How do we measure air temperature?

Air temperature is how hot or cold the air is. One way to measure this is with a **thermometer**. A thermometer measures how hot or cold the air is in degrees.

There are different kinds of thermometers, but they all share the same basic parts. They have a sensor that measures the temperature and a display that shows what that temperature is.

display

sensor

Why do we measure air temperature?

Air temperature is the aspect of the weather we measure most often. We use this information to help us forecast the weather. Air temperature affects other weather elements, such as wind speed and direction as well as rainfall.

It is important to protect yourself from the sun on a hot day.

Air temperature can tell us important information, such as whether there will be dangerous ice on roads. It can also tell us whether there will be heatwaves. Information about the temperature helps us predict plant and animal growth, health and wellbeing. It also helps us understand changing weather patterns.

It is dangerous to drive on icy roads, so preparing is important.

The Importance of Measuring

Measuring information about rainfall, wind speed, water levels and air temperature is very important. It helps us plan and stay safe. It sometimes helps us ease the impact of natural disasters, or at least be ready for them.

Sandbags can help stop a house from being flooded.

Measuring the weather gives us a bigger picture, too. It helps us understand current and changing weather patterns. This can help us plan for the future.

More people look up information about the weather on the internet than anything else.

Measuring

Instrument	What it measures	How it measures
Udometer	Rainfall	Monitors how much rain falls in a certain place for a certain amount of time
Satellite	Ocean water level	Measures the distance of radio waves bouncing between it and the ocean
Anemometer	Wind speed and gust	Rotates at the same speed as the wind
Weather vane	Wind direction	Points at the wind direction
Thermometer	Air temperature	Records how hot or cold air is in degrees

Glossary

anemometer: a tool for measuring wind speed

drought: a long period of time without any rain

gusts: strong bursts of wind

knot: a unit used to measure wind speed at sea

radio waves: electromagnetic waves used to transmit data

satellites: objects that orbit around the earth

shortages: when there is not enough of something

thermometer: a tool for measuring temperature

udometer: a tool for measuring rainfall

weather systems: movements of cold and warm air across the planet

Index